THE TIM⊕THY INITIATIVE

Disciples Making Disciples
Level 2

Edited by TTI Staff
November 2017
Version 1.01.18

2 Timothy 2:2

And the things you have heard from me among many witnesses, commit these to faithful men who will be able to teach others also.

TTI Contact Information:

admin@ttionline.org

<u>www.ttionline.org</u>

Acknowledgments

We would like to acknowledge and thank the following individuals, ministries, and resources for their godly character, leadership, insight, and inspiration which contributed to the formation of this manual:

Curtis Sergeant and George Patterson for their insight and counsel

Dave Watson and *Discovery Bible Study* Method

Dan Lachich and Northland Church's *Distributed Church Field Guide*

George Patterson and Richard Scoggins' *Church Multiplication Guide*

Van Velsor, McCauley, and Ruderman's *The Center for Creative Leadership Handbook of Leadership Development*

Table of Contents

Welcome to Disciples Making Disciples- Level 2

By the time you reached the completion of *Disciples Making Disciples- Level 1* you have led one or more people to Christ. At this point you need to answer the question, "What Next?" Based on your Level 1 training you realize every disciple is called to be a disciple maker. So, what are you going to do with your growing group of new disciples?

As mentioned at the end of Level 1, there are a few ways to go forward in the disciple making relationship. Some may choose to continue the discipleship relationship by encouraging new believers to join their existing church.

In some instances, connecting to an existing church may not be the best option. If this is your situation, we suggest that you begin gathering with your new believers on a regular basis as a smaller spiritual family under the banner and leadership of your existing church.

While you remain aligned and accountable to the common vision, mission, and leadership of your church, your group of new believers can begin meeting together in homes, offices, clubhouses, coffee shops, barber shops, etc.

The ultimate purpose of your gathering together is to make disciple making disciples.

Disciples Making Disciples- Level 2 will greatly assist you as you go forward in your discipleship journey and provide a guide and framework for developing your new and growing spiritual family into reproducing disciple makers.

Clarifying Terms

Micro church is a newer term without a lot of exposure or baggage in many Christian circles. When we refer to a **micro church** (or for short, "**MC**") in this training, we are simply describing an intentional gathering of disciples that happens outside the walls of a traditional or official church building.

A **micro church,** or **MC,** is simply a gathering of believers under the authority of Biblically qualified leadership, who meet regularly to worship the Father, study and communicate the Word of God in the power of the Holy Spirit, pray and fellowship together, observe the ordinances, and go out to share the love of Christ to the lost world with the intentionality to fulfill the Great Commission and multiply disciple makers.

These gatherings tend to be smaller in size and often meet in houses, offices, restaurants, clubhouses, or wherever is convenient for the group.

TTI also makes a distinction between "discipling" and "disciple maker." **Discipling** is viewed as helping existing believers grow in their faith, with an emphasis on Biblical knowledge, spiritual disciplines, engaging in serving others, and leading/encouraging others within the body of Christ.

Disciple makers are those who are involved in discipling, but are also engaged in intentional evangelism, bringing lost people to Christ, and leading them in relationships that result in reproduction of disciple makers.

Based on these definitions, this training is specifically designed for disciple makers.

Introduction
Setting the Stage for Mobilizing Disciple Makers

When Jesus said to go and make disciples, He was saying, "as you go, make disciples." He was not only suggesting His disciples needed to make disciples in places they were not, but also wherever they were or would be.

Making disciples is something for every believer, not just a minister or pastor. At the same time, we remember Jesus is the One with all the authority, and it is His presence that empowers our work (*Matthew 28:19-20*). Not clinging to His authority and to His presence will always result in failure.

Making disciples also happens best in relationship. Oftentimes the people most influenced and impacted by our story (the way Jesus changed us) and God's story are those with whom we are already in relationship. Those we meet for the first time can be equally impacted, however. The main point is to begin with those who respond to the Gospel! These can be friends, family, neighbors, colleagues, classmates, and those we encounter in the places we live, work, study, shop, and play.

In order to bring the church closer to the lost world, so they can witness the transformational power of the Gospel, we need to be the church outside the four walls of a building (*Romans 1:16*). Furthermore, when people encounter Jesus and are compelled by what they see and feel, sending them back to a central building may not always be appropriate or most natural.

TTI believes in traditional and non-traditional forms of church, both inside and outside of buildings. We must accept the reality that we may need to offer people the option to join a community of believers that does not require attendence to an actual building or highly structured ministry.

Just think, what percentage of the population can the existing church buildings in your community hold at a given time? The answer is likely less than 20% of any population center.

The point here is not to abandon the existing structure of church, but to offer additional solutions or tracks to those who are unable or uninterested in entering our buildings. For example, many people work on Sundays, speak different languages, have transportation issues, cannot attend due to family pressures, or are turned off by organized religion.

At present, the reality in many places remains that **if they don't enter our buildings, they don't encounter our message.** Just as the church is organized inside the building, it should be organized outside as well.

Arranging our lives around Jesus happens best in the context of community and relationships. In Jesus' community (the church) we observe and learn to obey all that Jesus commanded us. This means the church exists for the purpose of glorifying God by bringing people to Christ, and making them into "little Christs," sent wherever they are to make disciples. This way, whether inside or outside a building, the message of the Gospel of Jesus is making its way to those who need to hear it most.

What must we overcome?
Disciple making is not something we do alone. It requires accountablity and transparancy. It is a conformation and commitment to a way of life that includes others. It is so much more than gathering together for a few hours a week

on a particular day. It is a lifestyle marked by obedience and intentionality to fulfilling the Great Commission.

Guiding Principles

As we continue this journey, it is important that we are clear on the expectations of this training and the basic pattern of disciple making and church planting established by the early church.

There are three key passages that can serve as an overview for the pattern of disciple-making and church planting in the New Testament.

1. Evangelism: *Acts 13:1-14:28*
2. Establishing: *1 Timothy 3:14-16*
3. Empowering: *Ephesians 4:11-16*

In each of these three areas, certain functions take place:

Evangelism: The Gospel spreads between family and friends, across neighborhoods, schools, and workplaces as the Holy Spirit works though the faithful and intentional pursuit of disciples. The church is also a witness in the community as the hands and feet of Christ as it models for all to see authentic relationships centered on loving others and obeying the commands of Christ.

Establishing: The church is established in the faith through a commitment to be led by the Holy Spirit and Holy Scriptures. New believers are engaged and expected to live out their faith, grow in relationships, and live a life that follows in the footsteps of Jesus. Every disciple understands they have been entrusted with gifts and abilities to contribute to the local church and Kingdom expansion. It is clear to all that the church exists for the purpose of discipleship.

Empowering: The church intentionally develops leaders to provide oversight and spiritual direction to the community of believers. Leaders are identified, trained, and empowered for the shepherding of the church.

Key Principle: All training happens in ministry, not just for ministry.

Setting the Stage

As we go forward, we are going to be looking at starting a disciple making movement. It is exciting! It is messy! It is rewarding! It is something God desires from His children.

Chapter 1- Introduces best practices and lays the foundation for creating a healthy disciple making culture.

Chapter 2- Provides a simple and reproducible pattern for disciple makers to discover the Bible together.

Chapter 3- Answers basic questions for starting simple and reproducible micro churches.

Chapter 4- Shows how to start micro churches.

Chapter 5- Shows how to reproduce micro churches.

Chapter 6- Introduces an effective and intentional discipleship process.

Chapter 7- Describes balanced discipleship that results in spiritual maturity.

Chapter 8- Shows how mentoring is critical to the process of equipping and developing leaders.

Chapter 9- Covers defining marks of success and key areas for evaluation and accountability.

Chapter 1
Best Practices to Follow Throughout the Training

Expected Outcome: Every disciple maker will assess, challenge, and support their disciple makers.

At the outset of your training we would like to offer some general guidelines and best practices to assist you in this training. The following is based on extensive research in leadership development and practical ministry experience from around the world. We also invite you to begin thinking through your own context specific realities and strategies to employ as you continue this journey.

Assess, Challenge, & Support Your Disciple Makers

The following serves as a simple framework to help you throughout this training to put your disciples in the best possible scenario to succeed.

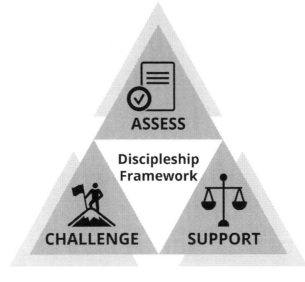

***You will be seeing this ACS logo throughout this manual. Anytime you see it, your Paul will pause to model and give a chance for you to practice so that you are clear on the principle, and ready to transfer it to your disciples.

The following explains ACS*

<u>Assess:</u> encourage practical activities and assignments that are clearly defined and easily measurable. It is important to understand where your disciples are and how to engage and motivate them to higher levels of growth.

<u>Challenge:</u> everything should be appropriately challenging to the individual and connected back to strengthening, learning, and growing in knowledge and practice. Activities and assignments should be tailored to fit the level of the disciple so they are challenging but not setting them up for failure.

<u>Support:</u> everything you ask others to do should be balanced by reasonable levels of support. You must be a source of encouragement and help throughout the development process.

Intentionally and Tangibly Develop your Disciple Makers

As you see on the next page, there are 4 stages or levels that each disciple progresses through on their journey of development and growth. Using the ACS framework you will move disciples through the stages as they master skills, concepts, and abilities.

*ACS adapted from Van Velsor, McCauley, and Ruderman's *The Center for Creative Leadership Handbook of Leadership Development*

TTI's Leadership Development Circle

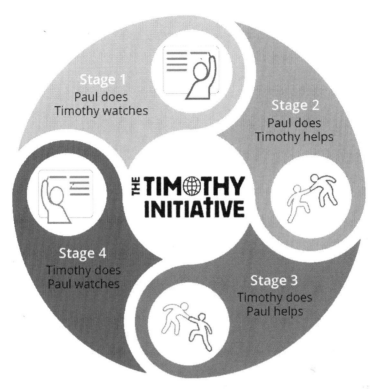

Stage 1: focuses on modeling to your disciples exactly what to do, how to do it, and why you do it the way that you do.

- **The mere transfer of knowledge or teaching of truths is never enough to make disciple making disciples.**

Stage 1 Goal: Use every occasion to model and practice is as an opportunity to move Timothys through the different stages of development.

Stage 2: focuses on continuing to model the ideas, skills, techniques, or strategies required to become effective at a particular task.

- **Skill modeling may seem like a foreign concept when it comes to discipleship but is critical to development!**

12

- Jesus regularly modeled this with his disciples (*Matthew 14:13-21; Mark 9:30-50; Luke 10; John 20:30*). This gives everyone a chance to get their feet wet without the weight of the consequences on their shoulders.
- Consider for a moment any profession where the lives of people are potentially at risk (doctor, pilot, etc.). They undoubtedly use some sort of residency, internship, or apprenticeship for those new to the trade. On-the-job training is required and practical knowledge and skills must be displayed before they can take up the profession on their own.

Stage 2 Goal: Providing practical and simple opportunities gives the "hours" required to learn what to do, how to do it, and why it should be done. Empower early and often, letting your Timothys know you are there to help as needed.

Stage 3: looks to challenge and empower your disciples, while at the same time supporting them with your presence and help.
- Oftentimes we see in Scripture the disciples working while Jesus takes a back seat, helping whenever it is needed (*Mark 9:14-21*).

Stage 3 Goal: Help your Timothy learn to stand on his/her own. Your presence alone is a source of strength and encouragement. Feel free to support and assist in a way that does not undermine their abilities or hinder their growth.

Stage 4: releases the disciple to stand on their own and establishes them in a way that they have the confidence necessary to successfully tackle their relevant task.
- Whether it be sharing one's faith, explaining a verse or Bible story, praying publically, or any other

13

practical and simple task required of a disciple maker, it is important you see your people through all four stages.

- Jesus did not give his disciples a polished church manual and say "follow these rules for a flawless church." He modeled who they needed to be and what they needed to do in order to start a movement that will ultimately fulfill the Great Commission. Follow His example! As you do, your disciples will follow (*1 Cor. 11:1*).

Stage 4 Goals: Celebrate successes and encourage them by articulating ways you have seen them grow. Explain how the mastering of one skill reveals the need to master others. Encourage a posture of life-long learning, growing, and developing as a Christ follower and disciple maker.

Model & Practice #1

Your Paul will now take time to explain and model exactly how they have tried to move you through the Leadership Development Circle in the past, and what they are doing presently to get you to the next stage.

- Break up into smaller groups and practice with each other. The goal is to practice this in your own life so you can do this with your disciples. Consider specific tasks or skills and where your disciples are at in the developmental process and how you can move them forward using the ACS framework.

The Essential DNA &
Core Values of Effective Disciple Makers

When it comes to creating a unified vision and shared core values, we have found the following to be critical to the success of seeing and sustaining a movement of disciple makers and church planters. Continually return to these core values and essential DNA of all disciple makers:

1. **Kingdom Focus**: It's all about the Kingdom! This truth gives purpose to our lives and relationships, shapes our values and behaviors, and directs our desires and focus.

2. **Spirit-Led and Scripture-Based**: The Holy Spirit and The Holy Scriptures are our guides in everything we do.

3. **Integrity First**: God values integrity and expects it in all we do.

4. **Every Believer is a Disciple and Every Disciple is called to be a Disciple Maker**. The best way to grow the church is to make disciples.

5. **Prayer is Priority**: Prayer cannot be separated from planning and acting.

6. **All People Matter**: Consistently ask God to burden our hearts and give us an urgency to reach the world.

7. **Faith Driven**: We want to bring glory to God in all we do. Our success depends upon His favor. He wants us to trust Him.

Chapter 2
Discovering the Bible Together

Expected Outcome: Every disciple maker will lead a group to discover the Bible together.

As you begin regularly gathering with your disciples, you will want to encourage them in their walk with Christ. Keeping in mind the **Best Practices to Follow Throughout the Training** (Chapter 1), we suggest a simple, reproducible, and practical way to train and equip disciple makers through the Bible. The following outline highlights exactly how to make this happen.

Prayer

Before you discover the Bible together, go around the room and have everyone share one thing they are **thankful for** and one thing that is causing **anxiety, fear, or stress**. Emphasize to the group that one aspect of prayer is just telling God the things we are thankful for and talking with Him about what worries or stresses us out.

Encourage a time of collective prayer so that all who desire have a chance to pray for the group members. This form of prayer is very interactive and should hopefully get even the quietest people involved in group prayer.

Note: Even if someone was invited for the first time and is not yet a follower of Christ, encourage them to join you in this process of prayer and reflection. As your group grows, it is important to remember that prayer must expand beyond just the group needs. Worship is also a natural outcome of believers gathering together.

The Holy Spirit

Right after you pray, ask the group to share how God spoke to them in their personal time with Him (daily devotions) since your last meeting. **Asking these questions at the beginning of every meeting reinforces the imortance of personal quality time with God. It also affirms an expectation of accountability, while at the same time validating every individual's ability to hear God's voice.**

This is the time to ask each person how they did with the previous weeks commitments, assignments, and their *I WILL* statements. Did they follow through with what they committed? What were the results? What challenges are they facing and what course corrections need to be made?

Giving an opportunity for everyone to share allows room for the Holy Spirit to take the group in the direction He desires. Be sensitive to the leading of the Holy Spirit and make sure all who desire have time to share.

Scripture

This section follows a similar pattern as the personal Bible study method outlined in Chapter 7 of Level 1.

Step 1: Read a passage of Scripture out loud while everyone follows along in their Bible or device (or listen carefully, for those without Bibles). The end of this book includes recommended passages to start with.

Step 2: Ask someone else to re-read the same passage out loud. This time have everyone listen to the reading (instead of following along).

Step 3: Ask another volunteer to retell the passage in their own words.

17

Step 4: Ask the group to fill in any points they feel were left out by the person retelling the story.

Note: It may seem repetititve or time consuming, but reading, listening, and retelling Scripture reinforces the importance placed on every disciple being anchored to and sustained by the Word of God.

This pattern also allows different learning styles to engage and interact with Scripture. Everyone has time to think about the passage and ask the Holy Spirit to speak through God's Word.

Retelling the passage in your own words models and allows everyone to think through how they can share this passage with someone from outside the group. Allowing the group to add to the retelling encourages everyone to think about the main points in the passage. **If they are not able to articulate the story in their own words, it is unlikely they will share it with others!**

Discovery Study

Step 5: After someone in your group retells the Scripture, you can study the passage. Your discussion should be filled with questions. Questions encourage and facilitate the discovery process. Questions allow your group to deeply consider Scripture and grow spiritually.

Below are some sample questions to encourage interaction with Scripture:
- What captured your attention in this passage?
- What did you like about this passage?
- Did anything bother you? Why?
- What does this passage tell us about God?
- What does this passage tell us about Man?

- What does this passage tell us about living to please God?
- Is there a command to obey or an example to follow?
- Is there a principle to apply or sin to avoid?
- If there are people who don't yet know Christ, this may be an opportunity for them to accept Christ.

Note: Keep discussion focused on Scripture and try to limit the discussion of extra-Biblical or outside materials. These materials are not bad, but they don't facilitate interaction with Scripture. The goal is to discover God's Word together and to create a reproducible process so others can do the same!

Prayer & Commitment (*I WILL* Statements)

Step 6: Knowledge of God's Word must translate into obedience or it is wasted. Take five minutes for everyone to pray silently and ask the Lord how He wants them to respond and with whom they should share with this week. This step ends with a question:

"Since we believe God's Word is true, what must we do or change in our lives to obey God?"

Everyone in the group should answer this question before they leave. In a sense, these questions help reveal the *I WILL* statements for each individual. If they already obey this Scripture, have them share how they obey it. Ask them if there is anything else they need to do to increase their obedience to God's Word in this area of their life. Keep this part of your time focused on specifics not generalities.

For example, realizing that there is only one God is great, but how does that lead to action? In this case you might encourage them with a follow up question: "Now that you believe there is one God, what do you need to do or change in your life?" Encourage your group to identify specific I WILL statements in order to obey the passage.

As the leader of the group, ask everyone to write down their own commitments and *I WILL* statements. Make sure to also ask for permission to write down everyone's response to hold them accountable at the next gathering

Step 7: After everyone shares how they are going to obey Scripture, have them identify someone who needs to hear what God said to the group, or with whom the Lord is leading them to share the Gospel.

Encourage them to share what they learned with that person and hold them accountable to do so. Before you finish, ask the group to identify people they know who are in need. Ask the group to specify ways they can meet those needs in the next week. Finally, close in a prayer of commitment.

Checklist for Discovering the Bible Together

Laying the Foundation- Prayer & Holy Spirit
- Begin by having the group share one thing they are thankful for and one challenge that is stressing them out in a group prayer process.
- Ask the group to share what God told them in their daily devotions since the last gathering.
- Ask them to share how they were obedient to the previous week's Scripture and who they shared with.

7 Steps to Discovering the Bible Together

Step 1: Read (or listen to) the week's portion of Scripture out loud while people follow along in their Bibles.

Step 2: Have someone else read (or play) the same passage out loud while the group listens.

Step 3: Ask someone else to retell the passage in their own words.

Step 4: Allow the group to correct or add any points they feel were left out by the person retelling the story.

Step 5: Use discovery questions to encourage the group to interact with the passage.
- What captured your attention in this passage?
- What did you like about this passage?
- Did anything bother you? Why?
- What does this passage tell us about God?
- What does this passage tell us about Man?
- What does this passage say about living to please God?
- Is there a command to obey or an example to follow?
- Is there a principle to apply or sin to avoid?
- If there are people who don't yet know Christ, ask: "Does anyone want to accept Christ?"

Step 6: Prayer & Commitment- Challenge the group to obey God's Word.
- Take five minutes for everyone to pray silently and ask the Lord how He wants them to respond and what they should do this week.
- "Since we believe God's Word is true, what must we do or change in our lives to obey God?"
- Have each person share their *I WILL* statements focusing on what they are going to do to obey the passage over the next week.
- Record their answers.

Step 7: Have the group identify people they will share the passage with during the next week and write down their names.
- Try to identify people in need within your community and commit to meeting tangible needs. Close in a prayer of commitment.

Doesn't this method get old or repetitive?
The way we lead a lesson is almost as important as the lesson itself. We can chose to use teaching techniques that build a listeners dependence on a "teacher." Or, we can use techniques that prepare a listener to stand on their own from the beginning. The repetition is intentional. We desire that all participants (after only a few lessons) see this process as easy and reproducible. **Repitition aids reproduction.**

The goal is ultimately that each Timothy is confident and able to lead and facilitate their own MC through this discovery process. Your Paul will move you through the stages of leadership until you can do this on your own.

Closing Thoughts
The above is a simple and practical approach to use whenever you meet together with your disciples. The steps are clear, and the process is consistent and predictable. The outcomes, however, are dynamic. The Bible is living and active (*Hebrews 4:12*). It is often called a sword, and serves as our best tool for defeating the enemy. Every disciple maker can use this process both personally and as they begin meeting with others.

For a detailed explanation, watch the short clip "*Discovery Group Process*" by CityTeam (http://youtu.be/dHggzCWYL-Q)

Model & Practice #2
Your Paul will now take time to model exactly how to discover the Bible together in a group, using a sample lesson from *Genesis 1:1-25.*

- Remember, the goal is to practice so you can do this with your disciples.

Recommended *Discovery Bible Study* Lessons to Start With

1. God Creates- *Genesis 1:1-25*
2. God Creates Man and Woman- *Genesis 2:4-24*
3. Man and Woman Eat the Fruit- *Genesis 3:1-13*
4. God's Curses- *Genesis- 3:14-24*
5. God Regrets His Creation- *Genesis 6:5-8*
6. God Saves Noah and his Family- *Genesis 6:9-8:14*
7. God's Covenant with Noah- *Genesis 8:15-9:17*
8. God's Covenant with Abram- *Gen. 12:1-8, 15:1-6, 17:1-7*
9. Abraham Gives his Son as an Offering- *Genesis 22:1-19*
10. God Spares His People- *Exodus 12:1-28*
11. The Commands of God- *Exodus 20:1-21*
12. The Sin Offering- *Leviticus 4:1-35*
13. God's Righteous Servant- *Isaiah 53*
14. Jesus is Born- *Luke 1:26-38, 2:1-20*
15. Jesus is Baptized- *Matthew 3; John 1:29-34*
16. Jesus is Tested- *Matthew 4:1-11*
17. Jesus and the Religious Leader- *John 3:1-21*
18. Jesus and the Samaritan Woman- *John 4:1-26, 39-42*
19. Jesus and the Paralyzed Man- *Luke 5:17-26*
20. Jesus Calms the Storm- *Mark 4:35-41*
21. Jesus and the Man with Evil Spirits- *Mark 5:1-20*
22. Jesus Raises a Man from the Dead- *John 11:1-44*
23. Jesus Talks about His Betrayal and the Covenant- *Matthew 26:17-30*
24. Jesus is Betrayed and Faces Trial- *John 18:1-19:16*
25. Jesus is Crucified- *Luke 23:32-56*
26. Jesus is Resurrected- *Luke 24:1-35*
27. Jesus Appears to the Disciples and Ascends to Heaven- *Luke 24:36-53*
28. Enter into the Kingdom God- *John 3:1-21*

*Important Note: More *Discovery Bible Study* lessons are listed in the back of this book.

Chapter 3
Some Basic Questions on Starting Micro Churches

Expected Outcome: Every disciple maker will identify where to plant micro churches.

Key Verses:
Matthew 28:18-20, Matthew 16:18, Romans 15:20

1. Why should we plant MC's?

Everywhere the apostles went, little bodies of believers sprung up! The directive of the Great Commission requires that we be disciples who make disciples. This is the best way for fulfilling the task of the Great Commission.

How does this practically happen?

It happens wherever we are and wherever we are going, by sharing the Gospel of Jesus, baptizing those who respond, and teaching them to obey all that He commanded. This is the mission of every gathering of disciples.

Consider the beginning of the Great Commission: He has all the authority needed for us to make disciples (*Matthew 28:18*). Remember, it is Jesus who said "I will build my church." In addition, He tells us that His presence will always be with us, "to the end of the age" (*Matthew 28:20*). Not clinging to His authority and to His presence will always lead to failure!

So, what is a micro church? How do we define an MC?

In the times of Jesus, 'ekklesia' was a familiar term. It was when the king met with his council of ministers or elders. They would get their marching orders during these meetings and gatherings. The Greek word 'ekklesia' is better-translated "assembly" or "congregation." In Level 1 we said a micro church is simply a spiritual family, with Christ in their midst as King, who love God, love others, and multiply disciples.

A micro church is not a building, but a gathering of believers.

The apostles obeyed Jesus by going from place to place, preaching the Gospel, planting churches, and appointing leaders (elders) in every place. This is the example we follow from the founding fathers of the early church.

2. Where should we plant MC's?

This is a major question you have to address when you think of planting a new **MC**. Below are some basic principles that can serve as a guide:
- **Plant MC's where there are no churches or MC's.**
- **Plant MC's in a specific community or neighborhood where people are not being effectively discipled.**

Is there a place in your neighborhood, city, county, district, or state where people are not being made into disciple makers? **Starting first with friends and relatives, followed by receptive individuals is generally the most effective approach. Don't be afraid to move on when people do not respond.**

One of the principles that guided the Apostle Paul was *Romans 15:20, "And so I have made it my aim to preach the Gospel, not where Christ was named, lest I should build on another man's foundation."* We need to plant MC's where there is no intentional and effective Gospel presence.

You may say, "There are so many churches in my city

already." Praise the Lord for your city, but we need to look at things in the light of the Great Commission. Is there a place in your sphere of influence where disciples are not being effectively made into disciple makers?

Is there a specific neighborhood that does not have a church? Is there a nursing home, rehab center, half way house, prison, or juvenile facility without a disciple making MC? What about a community of immigrants or people of other cultures who will not feel comfortable attending a more traditional church?

Is there a particular demographic that is not being effectively reached in your city or county? Is there a language group that does not have a church? Is there a particular part of society or sub-culture that needs to be targeted? For example, businessmen, professionals, medical workers, lawyers, students, gamers, taxi drivers, day laborers, athletes, homeless, etc.

If so, there is still a role for new MCs in your area. One great way to start is by taking prayer walks in the area you sense God leading you. Prayer walking while looking for persons of peace is similar to what happened in *Luke 10*.

 ## Model & Practice #3
Your Paul will now show you how they are doing this and then work with each individual, pair, or group to identify where to start their MC.

- Before moving on, plan out the next steps for where each MC is looking to start. Consider beginning with your own neighborhood, home, and new believers, and work out from there.

3. Who can and should plant MC's?

To answer this question, we would like you to answer another question. Who planted the Antioch church? Was it Paul, Peter, or Barnabas?

The answer is, none of them! It was started by scattered believers from Jerusalem who were so vibrant that communities of believers blossomed wherever they went. (See *Acts 11:19-21.*)

That is how we need to view every follower of Christ, including new believers! Rather than asking him/her to just listen and learn, each one also needs to be encouraged to go and make disciples. **Every follower of Christ has the potential to plant an MC.**

Many precious followers of Christ are not using their talents, gifts, and energies because they have not been released for Kingdom work. In the New Testament church, the expectation was that every follower of Christ was an active witness with the DNA of self-multiplication. The church should be like a starfish. If a star fish is cut into five pieces, it becomes five starfish. In other words, every obedient disciple of Jesus has the potential of becoming a self-multiplying disciple maker.

You may remember this from Level 1:

Every follower of Christ is a disciple.
Every disciple a disciple maker.
Every disciple's home a potential church.
Every church a potential church planting training center.

Every healthy MC should be planting new MC's in order to remain healthy. We will look at reproducing MC's in the last chapter.

4. What types of MC's should we plant?

God uses numerous ways, and people are diverse. We should respect all models of churches with their intrinsic advantages and disadvantages. God's desired outcome is more important than any specific model.

It is important that we ask ourselves whether or not the MC's we plant will themselves be reproducible. Will they have the DNA of multiplication?

5. How do we plant MCs?

Planting and multiplying MC's is easy if we just commit to following the example of Jesus and the early church. They must be simple enough to reproduce and yet still grow in health and maturity. But, how? Interestingly enough, you may have already started. We will dig deeper into how to start micro churches in the next chapter.

Additional questions to consider as you evaluate what it will take to reach the lost in your area.

What is your chosen place of ministry or location for your MC?

What are the distinct features and social networks of your area?
- Population
- Sub-cultures & Common Interests
- Languages Spoken
- Urban or Rural
- Economic Level
- Openness to the Gospel

What vision has God given you for this place?

How many MC's need to be started? How many MC's do you plan to start?

How many leaders need to be trained? How many leaders will you train, and who are you accountable to?

What is your plan for your chosen field for the next...
- Six Months
- One year
- Two years
- Number of MC's to be planted
- Number of disciple makers to be developed
- Number of neighborhoods evangelized

How will you disciple new Christ-followers?

Chapter 4
Starting Micro Churches

Expected Outcome: Every disciple maker will start Micro Churches.

Amplify vs. Simplify

It is important to start this chapter by defining a micro church. There are two main values competing against each other when starting micro churches. The first is the desire to teach well and cover all the bases (amplify). The second is to keep things as simple as the apostles did when they started (simplify). During the startup stage, it's the time to simplify. Amplify later. Let baby believers and baby micro churches be infants and drink milk. Patience is critical!

For those who like to simplify: A micro church is simply a spiritual family, with Christ in their midst as King, who love God, love others, and multiply disciples.

For those who like to amplify: A micro church is a gathering of believers under the authority of Biblically qualified leadership, who gather regularly to worship the Father, study and communicate the Word of God in the power of the Holy Spirit, pray and fellowship together, observe the ordinances, and go out to share the love of Christ to the lost world with the intentionality to fulfill the Great Commission and multiply disciple makers.

Let us break down the starting of MC's into sizeable chunks:
- Biblically qualified leadership
- Gather together regularly as a spiritual family
- Worship God, pray, fellowship & discover the Word of God in the power of the Holy Spirit
- Observe the ordinances
- Go out, sharing the love of Christ to the world
- Intentionally multiply disciples

 Biblically Qualified Leadership

Every MC will have a unique connection and relationship back to an existing body of believers (church or network of micro churches). While you remain aligned and accountable to the common vision, mission, and leadership of your church, your group of new believers will form something new...what we call a micro church.

If you look at the way New Testament churches formed, there was always a connection back to some spiritual father or leadership. In *1 Timothy 3* and *Titus 1*, Paul outlined some of the basic expectations for those who would lead a body of believers. Paul told Titus (*1:5*) to "put what remained in order" by appointing elders across the island of Crete. In Ephesus, he told Timothy what was expected of those who aspire to oversee the chuch (*1 Timothy 3*).

Nearly all micro churches in an expanding movement are started when the head of a family receives Jesus and starts shepherding his family from day one. Friends and relatives join this nucleus of a home church. Early on there is usually a time when no one qualifies as a "proven" shepherding elder, so non-proven provisional leaders shepherd their family and friends in the meantime, until they can be recognized as a qualified elder, with laying on of hands and sending out (*Acts 13:3*).

In the context of this training, your Paul represents Biblically qualified and spiritual leadership (not every MC needs identified and offical elders). Whatever that relationship looks like, it is important that there be clear expectations on both sides what your role is when it comes to oversight, accountability, and authority.

Practical Questions to Answer:
- Who am I accountable to?

- Am I willing to submit to my identified spiritual leaders?
- Do I measure up to the expectations outlined in *1 Timothy 3* and *Titus 1*?

Model & Practice #4.1

Based on the questions above, your Paul will discuss the practicalities of Biblically qualified leadership within an MC.

- Each Timothy will need to work with their Paul to better identify areas of strength and weakness, where they are at in their growth and development, and where they must grow in order to meet expectations.

Gather Together Regularly

At this point in the training, you have already been intentional about praying for the lost and seeking the direction of the Holy Spirit. You have been consistently sharing your story and God's story with those God is leading you to. It is a natural next step to begin regularly meeting with your new disciples who have come to Christ. Coming together with this purpose in mind is a great way to establish an MC.

One of the best ways to assess, challenge, and support your disciple making efforts is to gather together with your disciples on a regular basis. The "when" and "where" are less important than <u>what</u> you do when you gather and <u>why</u> you do what you do.

You should establish a consistent and intentional rhythm of gathering together with the purpose of:

- Ensuring disciples have the spiritual stamina to remain faithful, available, and teachable in the midst of life's trials.
- Looking back on what God has done and is doing.
- Reflecting on God's greater purposes and plans.
- Reinforcing essential DNA of disciples making disciples.
- Making course corrections and training more in tune with the Word of God and Spirit of God.

Practical Questions to Answer:

- When is a convenient time to meet on a regular basis?
- Where can you meet? **Once these two questions are answered, begin meeting!**

 # Model & Practice #4.2

Your Paul will now take time to show you how to do these things when you gather together (based on the above points).

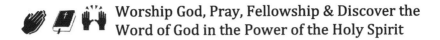 Worship God, Pray, Fellowship & Discover the Word of God in the Power of the Holy Spirit

Now that you have established a day, time, and location of where you are going to meet with your disciples, it is important to dig deeper into what you actually do when you meet. *Chapter 2* already outlined a very simple and reproducible way to effectively discover the Bible together. Following this approach will keep your group from becoming stagnant or distracted from worshiping God, praying together, fellowshiping together, and discovering the Word of God in the power of the Holy Spirit. The early church is a great example to follow in this regard.

Take a moment and look at what they did when they came together (*Acts 2:42-47*). Below we look to follow their model in a practical way.

<u>Worship</u>- The point here is to center our focus on God – who He is, and what He has done. A natural response to His greatness and goodness is awe and worship (*Acts 2:43, 47*). This can take many forms and will look different depending upon your context. Some people sing songs and hymns; others recite Scripture; others tell of the things God is doing and has done. The aim is to **look back on what God has done and is doing**. The natural response is worship! Do not feel any pressure to adopt worship styles from other traditions into your MC's.

<u>Prayer</u>- Every time you gather is a chance to pray. **Worship naturally leads to prayer—and prayer, to worship.** Before you begin studying the Bible together, take time to pray for each other and ask the Spirit of God to guide and direct your path (*Proverbs 3:5-6*). The early church devoted themselves to prayer, as they jointly shared a common vision and mission in obedience to God and the apostles teachings (*Acts 2:42*).

Fellowship- Connecting to each other in community – relationally and spiritually, is a vital aspect of any church. Ensure there is sufficient time for interaction, confession, and encouragement. The early church was together, sharing their time, talents, and money (sacrificially giving) as each had need (*Acts 2:44-45*). They also purposefully served one another and those in their community. They shared meals and communion with "*glad and generous hearts that praised God*" (*Acts 2:46*). One of the outcomes of this lifestyle was "*favor with all the people,*" as well as the Lord adding to their number daily (*Acts 2:47*)!

Practical Questions to Answer:
- How will you worship together as a group?
- How will you pray together as a group?
  - What if no one prays?
- How often should you share a meal and how often should you simply meet?
- Do you rotate locations so that one place does not get overburdened?
- How do you collect offerings in an MC?
  - How you do this is ultimately up to each MC. One simple method is to establish expectations that after "membership" into an MC, which is usually characterized by baptism, a regular offering be collected in order to meet the specific needs inside the MC (*Acts 2:44-45*) as well as your Jerusalem, Judea, Samaria, and ends of the earth (*Acts 1:8*).

 ## Model & Practice #4.3

Your Paul will now take time to show you how to do these things when you gather together (based on the above points).

<u>Discover the Word of God in the power of the Holy Spirit-</u>
Reflecting on God's greater purposes and plans always requires interaction with the Word of God and the Spirit of God. As you worship, pray, and fellowship together there must be an emphasis that reinforces the importance of daily devotions and self-feeding. This affirms every individual's ability to hear God's voice and respond accordingly.

The early church devoted themselves to the apostles teachings (*Acts 2:42*). Staying grounded in God's Word helps identify course corrections required to remain in obedience and provides deeper spiritual nourishment to grow in knowledge and action (*James 1:22-25*). A missionary once said "our challenge is to be inclusive in extending grace to all people yet exclusive in affirming that the Bible is the authoritative truth of God."

Practical Questions to Answer:
- Who will lead or facilitate the regular gathering?
- Who will lead the discovering the Bible portion of the gathering?
- Who will take notes regarding actions steps of each member?

*Important Note: Continue following the process of discovering the Bible as outlined in Chapter 2. This will keep you on track and in tune with the way God is moving your group. If helpful for the group, take time to review the key steps involved in the process.

This is a big chapter with a lot of information. Take time to ensure everyone is on the same page and ready for application!

Observe the Ordinances

Communion- Breaking bread together (sharing a meal) is a natural time to observe communion (*Acts 2:46*). As your MC looks back on what God has done, there is a natural response to idenfy the work of Jesus on the Cross and his sacrificial gift of life. Glad and generous hearts naturally remember the life, death, and resurrection of Jesus by observing communion (*1 Corinthians 11:23-25*).

Practical Question to Answer:
- Who will serve communion?
- What will I need to serve communion?
- How do you observe communion in an MC?
  - When you gather together, sharing a meal provides an opportunity to celebrate communion (*Acts 2:42-47*).
  - Follow the example of the last supper (*Matthew 26:26-28*) and that of the apostles (*1 Corinthians 11:23-26*).

Baptism is the other ordinance given to the Church which was modeled (*Matthew 3:13-27*) and commanded (*Matthew 28:19*) by Christ and His apostles (*Acts 2:38*). Baptism signifies the life, death, and resurrection of Jesus. *Romans 6:4 says "we were buried with Him through baptism into death, that just as Christ was raised from the dead by the glory of the Father, even so we also might walk in newness of life."*

Baptism is the outward expression of what God has done on the inside and provides a public declaration of faith and obedience. How you handle this will vary, but **there is always an expectation that obedience to the commands of Christ take precedence over tradition or cultural norms.**

Practical Questions to Answer:
- How do you conduct baptisms in an MC?
- How do you know when someone is ready for baptism? (Note: The apostles always baptized as the very first thing a new believer did, no exceptions. This powerfully affirms the new believer of his salvation and place in the body of Christ).
  - How you do this is ultimately up to each MC. There are many ways to go about conducting baptisms though. They can happen in an existing church building, local swimming pool (underground or inflatable), hot tub, or even a bathtub. The location is less important than the commitment to obey the command to follow up repentance and faith with baptism (*Acts 2:38-41*)!

*Important Note: **Baptism, communion, giving, and submission to local authority are unifying and help to create and reinforce a stronger group identity.** However your church leadership prescribes these functions should take place, remember that each MC is a family, and incorporating these functions and ordinances into the MC will empower, validate, and accelerate the group towards further growth and multiplication.

Model & Practice #4.4

Your Paul will now take time to show you how to observe the ordinances and cover any further questions you may have.

Go out, sharing the love of Christ to the world

The natural and expected response anytime a gathering of disciples takes place is a love for Christ and the world. God "desires all men to be saved and to come to the knowledge of the truth" (*1 Timothy 2:4*). He has entrusted his disciples with the ministry of reconciliation (*2 Corinthians 5:18*), and the mission of the Great Commission (*Matthew 28:19-20*). The Lausanne Committee for Word Evangelization sums it up well, saying, "the whole church is called to take the whole Gospel to the whole world, proclaiming Christ until He comes, with all necessary urgency, unity and sacrifice."

As each disciple is reminded of their personal responsibility to make disciples, there is a renewed compassion and love in their hearts, improved perspective of eternity in their minds, and greater intentionality to their walk!

Practical Questions to Answer:
- Is there an expectation following each gathering that every disciple is being sent out to share the love of Christ to the world?
  - For example, every disciple can share the love of Christ with at least one individual on a weekly basis.
- How will you hold each other accountable?

 ## Model & Practice #4.5
Your Paul will now take some time to discuss ideas and show you how to practically share the love of Christ with others.

Intentionally Multiply Disciples

The regular gathering of believers naturally serves as a time to reinforce the essential DNA of disciples making disciples. It has been said our mindset is the greatest indicator as to who or what we are allowing to lead us (*Romans 8*).

As you may have noticed, you have come full circle in the disciple making process. **Just as the gathering of disciples has naturally led to micro churches forming...the forming of micro churches should naturally lead to more disciple making.**

As a leader in the MC, your role is outlined in Ephesians 4 as an equipper of disciples for the work God has called them to do. This is a serious task and requires commitment, devotion, sacrifice, and a life marked by prayer and fasting.

Practical Questions to Answer:
- What do you do with disciples who seem uninterested in making disciples?
- How do you handle conflict within the MC?
- As disciples begin making more disciples the MC will grow. What happens when there is no more space?
- How soon should a disciple within the group be entrusted to launch a new group out of the MC?

 # Model & Practice #4.6
Your Paul will now take time to discuss and show you how to be an equipper of disciples.

Process of Starting Micro Churches

Biblically Qualified Leadership
Make sure you identify and remain accountable to local authority

Gather Together Regularly
Establish a time and place to meet regularly

Worship God, Pray, Fellowship & Discover the Word of God in the power of the Holy Spirit
When you gather, follow the discovering the Bible model which allows for worship, prayer, fellowship, giving, and commitment to being led by the Word and Spirit of God

Observe the Ordinances
Consistently follow public declarations of salvation with baptism and remember Christ through communion

Go out sharing the love of Christ to the world
Each meeting serves as a time to align and encourage disciples to the mission of the Great Commission and the ministry of reconciliation

Intentionally multiply disciples
Every believer is a disciple and every disciple is expected and held accountable to be disciple makers

Chapter 5
Reproducing Micro Churches

Expected Outcome: Every disciple maker will reproduce micro churches.

Reproducing Micro Churches

Whether you are a micro church, or prefer a different title, it is the hope and expectation that you consciously and consistently obey the commands of Christ by doing everything an obedient church would do. The smallness of your group allows for more intimate and purposeful application of the New Testament "one anothers."

As disciples are making disciples, the group will grow and reach a tipping point, where the decision to reproduce or stop growing must be made. A choice not to reproduce is a choice to focus inward instead of outward.

Just as the gathering of disciples has naturally led to micro churches forming, the forming of micro churches should naturally lead to more disciples being made. This is natural and the expected norm.

MC reproduction happens when one MC births another MC.

As an MC grows, there comes a time when the size of the group is too big for the existing location. Or, the MC may no longer be able to effectively give the attention needed to the growth and development of its members. Although there is no magic number, a group normally reaches its capacity at around 5-7 families or 7-15 adults. Ultimately, the relational dynamics, number of leaders, and other context specific variables play a major role in this decision.

It is important from the very beginning as you grow to consider what must be done to birth additional MC's. Launching new MC's is a natural response to disciples making disciples and will be required if you are going to effectively address the lostness in your area. Remember, the required resources for the harvest are often found in the harvest!

If those you lead to Christ do not have a strong relational or geographic connection back to an existing MC, help them start a new MC. This means you can be part of 2 MC's at the same time. One MC can be viewed as your spiritual family and the other MC is where you are discipling and mentoring the leader. In this way, every member of an MC can also be looking to be an MC mentor (more explained on this below).

It has been said, a church that focuses a significant part of its prayer, time, focus, energy, and funds to reproducing daughter churches will, within a generation, likely win ten times as many people to Christ when compared to focusing those energies inwardly.

Which better describes your gatherings?
1. Focus on obedience, evangelism, discipleship, and reproduction.
2. Focus on knowledge, protecting, programs, and sustaining.

The first one tends to be outward focused while the second is inward. A chain reaction of multiple generations of disciples and churches is required to reach the world today! **This requires an outward focus.**

As an MC leader, there is an expectation that you invest deeply in developing leaders and mentoring them in their walks with Christ. Just as you are looking to your spiritual leadership for accountability and guidance, your disciples now look to you. Delegating authority, releasing control, and empowering with responsibility are critical at this juncture.

The previous chapters have outlined the process of effective discipleship and developing leaders. It is within this progression that you will realize it is time to birth a new MC's. Reproducing and multiplying wisely is a big task and must be done prayerfully and carefully. Being able to achieve results through others is a completely different dynamic than doing things yourself. It takes a shift in the way you spend your time, requires additional skills, and ultimately a shift in values. All of this contributes towards an increase in development and can produce a pipeline of future MC leaders.

Build Leaders by Modeling Jesus

All throughout the New Testament there is the idea of imitating or following after Christ. Jesus said "follow me" on many occasions. Both Peter and Paul echoed this message and encouraged those they led to follow the example of Christ:

- *"Be imitators of Christ"* (*Eph. 5:1*).
- Christ left us an example... that we should follow in His steps (*1 Peter 2:21*).

One of the challenges today is people have a hard time relating the example of Christ into their practical lives. As a result, there is a clear disconnect between their life and that of Christ. Paul was addressing this issue in *1 Corinthians 4:15-16* where he noted that even though they had "countless tutors or caretakers," they did not have anyone to look up to or to imitate. As a result, he challenged them to imitate him as he imitated Christ (*1 Corinthians 11:1*). There is no greater example to others than offering your life as a model to follow.

When was the last time you modeled something? How did you do it? Was it purely through words or also actions? Did you teach your son to throw a ball by showing diagrams? Or teach your daughter to swim by watching instructional videos? In both cases, you likely showed them by modeling.

Throughout this training there have been many occasions where your Paul has intentionally modeled various skills or steps for you to follow. You can do the same with your disciples. It takes time and energy to progress from knowing to doing.

Model Jesus by challenging others to do what you do, as you follow Christ! Take a moment to see how Paul modeled this to the church of the Thessalonians (*2 Thessalonians 3:6-12*).

 ## Model & Practice #5
Your Paul will now take time to share how they have they have modeled skills and practices necessary for your growth and development.

- **Discuss as a group how each person is attempting to model Jesus to their disciples.**

Practical Ways to Reproduce MC's

One of the keys from the very beginning is to encourage every "head of household" to take up the role of discipling their family. Even new believers can consistently lead their spouse and children in prayer, read scripture together, talk about God and challenge the entire family to walk with Jesus. If someone is not willing to lead their own family, they are unlikely to lead others also. Encourage and empower those in your MC to do so.

Reproducing by Launching New MCs

From the very beginning it is good for you to encourage your MC to prayerfully and practically consider the lostness of your town, country and world (Acts 1:8). Understanding the great need for the Gospel to go out to every man, woman, and child must drive us to our knees in prayer and fasting.

Don't be afraid to ask if anyone within the MC is being led to a particular neighborhood, people, or sub-culture near or far away *(Acts 13:1-3)*. Be willing to release and empower as the Holy Spirit guides. Ask if any of the other MC members would be willing to join them as they look to go out and start a new MC elsewhere. Remember to emphasize simple, loving, childlike obedience *(see example 1)*.

- Sometimes the best people may even be called to a new area. It will be painful to see them go (*1 Thessalonians 2:17-20*), but ultimately the expansion of the Gospel and obedience to Christ requires it!

Reproducing by Mentoring & Mobilizing New Believers

As mentioned earlier in the chapter, when MC members lead others to Christ who do not have a strong relational or geographic connection back to an existing MC, it is better to help them start a new MC with their own network of friends, family, etc, as opposed to adding them to an existing MC.

Ideally, MC members will be part of 2 MC's at the same time. One MC viewed as a spiritual family and the other MC where they are discipling and mentoring emerging leaders *(see example 2)*.

- There will always be a tendency to hold onto your best leaders rather than mobilizing and empowering them to lead outside of your MC.

Example 1
Reproducing by Launching New MCs

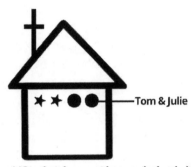

Tom and Julie started an MC in their home with a couple they led to Christ.

After six months, the group reached four more couples. Moved by the Holy Spirit, Mike and Denise feel led to start a new MC in a different part of town.

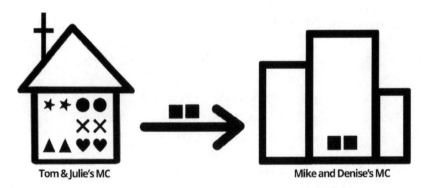

Tom and Julie's MC send out and empower Mike and Denise as they leave to plant a new MC in a different part of town.

Example 2
Reproducing by Mentoring & Mobilizing New Believers

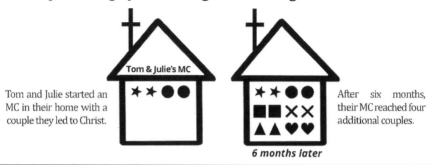

Tom and Julie started an MC in their home with a couple they led to Christ.

Tom & Julie's MC

6 months later

After six months, their MC reached four additional couples.

The group has become very close and view the MC as their spiritual family. As a result, they resist the idea of leaving this group to start another. With this in mind, Tom and Julie challenge group members to be part of two MCs, viewing one as their spiritual family and the other as where they are mentoring and mobilizing leaders. Group members Jimmy and Caroll take the challenge to heart, and begin praying about who they can mobilize to start a new MC. Their most recent convert Chris comes to mind as a great candidate.

Chris' New MC

Jimmy & Caroll *(mentors)*

Since Chris does not know anyone else in Tom and Julie's MC, Jimmy and Caroll decide to begin mentoring and discipling Chris and his spouse outside of their current MC. They encourage them to begin reaching out to their friends, neighbors, and coworkers to start an MC in their own home.

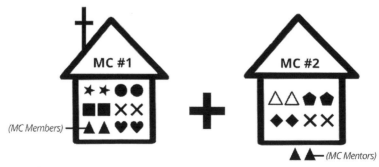

MC #1

(MC Members)

MC #2

(MC Mentors)

Jimmy and Caroll remain connected to their spiritual family and at the same time continue to mentor Chris and his wife in their new MC.

The main objective for this chapter is to reproduce MC's.
The Kingdom expands rapidly when every disciple has a spiritual family where they are growing and connecting, while at the same time, actively making disciple makers. As God's ambassadors this is who we are called to be and what we are called to do.

There is a time for praying, planning, and planting. By now it must be clear what steps you feel led to take. Things may not happen overnight, but don't delay scheduling a time to meet with your Paul to discuss how you will reproduce out of your MC.

As MC's reproduce, your responsibility of encouragement, commitment, and support never stops! Just as you desire to raise your natural children to maturity and adulthood, the same can be said for MC's. The remaining chapters focus on maturing, equipping, and developing what has begun into an even stronger movement of God. Never start something without the goal of seeing multiple generations!

Continue to model skills, pray together often, listen deeply, affirm strongly, all the while emphasizing simple, loving, childlike obedience to Christ. Faithfulness to the leading of the Spirit and the direction of Scripture always lead to spiritual fruit that remains. This must always remain the barometer of success. Remember, the defining marks of success for this training include:
- **Living in a love relationship with God.**
- **Growing continually as Christ-like leaders.**
- **Reproducing disciple making leaders.**
- **Planting multiplying MC's.**

Chapter 6
Effective Disciple Making

Expected Outcome: Every disciple maker will begin a balanced and reproducible disciple making process.

Key Verses: *Matthew 28:19-20, John 14:15-31, James 2:26*

Once you have led someone to Christ, it is natural for discipleship to begin wherever you may be. The expectations you place on these new believers will greatly impact their potential for multiplication. Every time new believers are added within a network of MC's, a decision must be made.

1. Gather them into an existing MC.

2. New believers launch a new MC out of an existing one.

The first of these choices is used most of the time. However, the second option represents far greater potential. Remember, every home should be viewed as a potential MC.

Establishing a Disciple Making Process

Consider the following seven questions as you begin to establish an intentional disciple making process.

First - is it based on obedience to Scripture?

It is not the amount of knowledge alone that makes a strong believer, but their degree of obedience. This is sometimes called *obedience based discipleship (John 14:15-31)*.

What do we obey?

The disciple maker does not only teach the commands of Christ. Rather, the disciple maker is to **teach obedience** to the commands of Christ and all of Scripture. Learning commands will never make healthy disciples. Blind legalism is not the result of obedience based discipleship. It is faithful obedience spurred on by love for God and people that sets a person on the right path. Obedience is the center of the Great Commission. The habit of obedience will serve the disciple throughout their life as they face new challenges.

Second - is it accountability based?

A life lived in obedience to Christ demands accountability. Part of Jesus' plan to save the world involved building a team, tasked with a mission. If you look at his example in *Luke 9-10*, Jesus prayed for who to invest in; He gave personal interaction (He chose them to be with Him), sent them out with authority, and finally, He held them accountable to report on what they had done.

While the idea of accountability may be counter-cultural, it is quite Biblical and an important ingredient to effective discipleship.

Third - is it providing responsibilities that challenge, empower, and support believers?

As *James 2:26* reminds us, "*Faith without works is dead.*" With this in mind, we should commission our disciples to the application of the Word. Empowering others with responsibility and supporting them throughout the process promotes rapid growth. Challenging new believers with manageable yet challenging tasks will accelerate their maturity. Grasping their own identity in Christ and their role in the body (MC) are the keys to them reaching their potential.

The best way to empower disciples is to encourage and show them what is expected of them. Remember TTI's leadership development circle which highlights practical ways to develop your disciples.

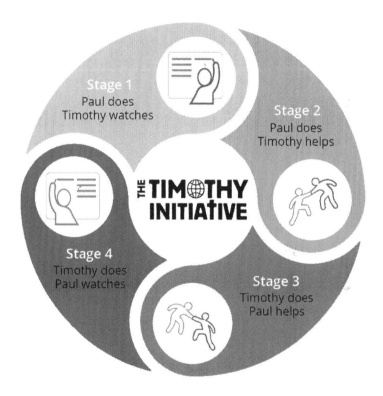

Fourth - does it promote and expect multiplication?

The greatest joy in ministry is not making disciples—it is seeing your disciples make disciples! In *2 Timothy 2:2*, Paul passes on a responsibility to Timothy.

Consider this key principle of discipleship: *"And the things that you have heard from me among many witnesses, commit these to faithful men who will be able to teach others also."*

Within this verse four generations of disciples can be observed.

1. Paul
2. Timothy
3. Reliable Workers
4. Others

The disciple maker must remember that everything needed for the harvest is in the harvest! A missionary once said "God's will, done God's way, never lacks God's supply." This includes the leaders promised to the church. (See *Ephesians 4:11-12.*)

The disciple maker must believe first-generation Christ-followers are capable of reaching, discipling, and mentoring others. When provided with appropriate tools, the gifts of even the newest Christ-followers can flourish.

Fifth - is it reproducible? (*2 Timothy 2:2*)

To ensure reproducibility, the disciple maker should use simple tools and systems. This process will prevent financial burdens or unavailable resources that often cripple the potential for multiplication.

Sixth - does it push believers toward self-feeding?
(*2 Timothy 3:16-17*)

The Word of God is designed to shape and sharpen every disciple. The truth of *John 14:26* still applies today. The Holy Spirit is still the Counselor. He is responsible for teaching the disciple of Christ all things and reminding him/her of the Words of Christ. There is a saying, "Give a man a fish, feed him for a day. Teach a man to fish, feed him for a lifetime." Are we giving fish, or training people how to catch fish? Which is better in the long run? (See *Mark 1:17*.)

Seventh - does it naturally lead towards the regular gathering of believers (MC's)? The natural result of discipleship leads towards MC formation, or at least it did in the New Testament.

With this in mind, every disciple making process should be evaluated to ensure an environment that flows freely into MC formation.

Keys to Effective Disciple Making

First - is it obedience based?
Second - is it accountability based?
Third - is it granting responsibilities that challenge, empower, and support believers?
Fourth - does it promote and expect multiplication?
Fifth - is it reproducible?
Sixth - does it push believers toward self-feeding?
Seventh - does it naturally lead towards the regular gathering of believers (MC's)?

Model & Practice #6

Your Paul will now take time to describe their own disciple making process and highlight examples of how they have moved people through the different stages of development.

- Take time to consider your own process of disciple making. Plot out where each of your new believers are in their development as believers and as disciple makers. How will you help them grow and move them to the next stage? Discuss.

Chapter 7
Disciple Making that Leads to Maturity

Expected Outcome: Every Disciple Maker will disciple and mentor in a way that leads to spiritual maturity.

Stop Asking The Wrong Questions

When it comes to discipleship, we often ask questions that leave us stuck. Generally we want to know how to do something in the sense of methodologies or techniques. The point here is not to suggest a strategy or method is negative, only to say that **it is disciples that make disciples, not materials.** There is no magic pill or secret formula. Authentic people, dependent on the Holy Spirit and grounded to the Holy Scriptures, is the common denominator.

Making disciples, according to Jesus, is simply teaching them to obey His commands.

There will be a tendency to ask questions like:
- How long will it take?
- How do I get them to change?
- What are the right steps for...?
- What are other successful people doing?

All of these questions feel natural and are appealing because they cost so little from us. They tend to elevate skills and systems over people. As a result, sole ownership to change is transferred to those struggling to address the problem. The outcome of this paradox is a lack of struggle to **work with people through problems.**

In most contexts of discipleship, there is a lot of teaching with very little learning or doing. **One suggestion we make** is to design your efforts in a way that supports learning and doing, even at the expense of teaching.

If life change is really the aim behind what we are doing, a steady, nuanced, and purposeful approach is preferred to a pre-determined plan. It has been said we need to value struggle over prescription, questions over answers, and tension over comfort.

It is important to understand that the Christian life is never static. The Christ-follower is to be constantly growing in both the knowledge and practice concerning the "Word of righteousness." (Hebrews 5:13)

The writer of Hebrews puts it this way, "*For everyone who partakes only of* **milk** *is unskilled in the Word of righteousness, for he is a babe. But* **solid food** *belongs to those who are of full age" (5:13-14).*

- Knowledge without practice produces pride and dryness.
- Practice without increased knowledge leaves one weak in the faith.
- Knowledge and Practice not imparted to the next generation dies in the generation it began with.

Both knowing and doing are necessary to begin and sustain growth as a disciple of Jesus Christ. Passing on what you are learning to others keeps the movement going. One helpful way to view discipleship is the metaphor of stairs. The vertical increase is added knowledge of God, man, and life as a Christ follower. The horizontal increase is knowledge applied and lived out in obedience to Scripture. Too much knowledge without application makes a stair case too steep to climb. At the same time, too much action without increased knowledge leaves one on a level plain. See the following chart that illustrates this dynamic.

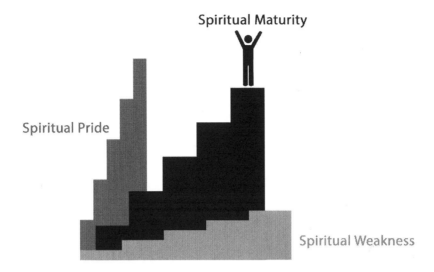

Spiritual Maturity

Spiritual Pride

Spiritual Weakness

Disciple Making Goals for the New Believer:
- Begin to understand their identity in Christ.
- Begin to develop loving obedience to the commands of Christ and establish a pattern of obeying without delaying.
- Begin to understand the role of the Holy Spirit in the life of every Christ-follower.
- Practice daily devotions and begin self-feeding.
- Begin sharing their story and God's story with their friends and relatives.
- Pass on everything they are learning to others
- Further training in the foundations of the faith and becoming engaged in evangelism and discipleship.
  - All of these topics are addressed in *DMD Level 1.*

In *Acts 2:37-47*, we see the first church, which was filled with new believers, following the commands of Christ. They include:
- Repentance and Faith – *v. 38*
- Baptism – *v. 41*

57

- Observance of the Lord's Supper – *v. 42, 46*
- Love for God and Others (expressed in service and fellowship)- *v. 42*
- Prayer – *v. 42*
- Giving – *v. 45*
- Making Disciples (Great Commission) – *v. 38, 47*

While this list does not include every one of Christ's commands, it does a good job at summing them up in order to teach the habit of loving obedience. All new disciples can be expeceted to do the same.

All of this will likely require that you show them what to do. Challenge, empower, and support disciples through the leadership circle and ensure a balanced stair step approach to learning and doing.

We recommend you engage a newly born disciple to obey these general commands of Christ right from the start. The goal is to establish an active, obedience-oriented MC, which is the essence of Biblical discipleship. We must lay this foundation of obedience in every new believer, just as Jesus emphasized in His conclusion to the sermon on the mount.

Model & Practice #7.1

Your Paul will now take time to explain how to follow a balanced stair step approach to learning and doing that results in spiritual maturity.

Disciple Making Goals for the Maturing or Mature Believer:
In addition to the goals for new believers, maturing and mature believers can look to go deeper in their faith in the following ways:
- Learn to walk in the Spirit and take captive every thought.

- Discover and enjoy a life in the church filled with spiritual fruit.
- Consistently share their story and God's story.
- Active involvement in mentoring and making disciples.
- Understand and experience the establishing, leading, and multiplying of an MC.

It is our experience that discipleship happens best in one-to-one or one-to-few relationships: ladies with ladies, and men with men. One effective way is to divide your MC into groups of twos/threes. These groups should include one Christ-follower who is more mature in the faith than the others. Allow time each week during (or outside) the normal MC meetings for these groups to connect. The purpose of this time is as follows:

- Accountability concerning obedience to the Scripture you have been discussing or covered in daily devotions.
- Discussion concerning the pre-Christians each person is praying for and desiring to share with.
- Prayer and encouragement for the challenges and needs in their lives.

The goal of these smaller groups is to grow by adding new Christ-followers that they have led to faith in Christ. Once additional persons are added, you then divide back into groups of twos/threes and repeat the process. These groups make themselves available to each other outside of the MC for prayer, support, evangelism and further discipleship. In this method, every member of your MC can be in a direct and personal discipleship relationship.

Model & Practice #7.2

Your Paul will now take time to help you evaluate and adjust your current methods to line up with those taught in this chapter.

For those who are not already involved in the process of intentional disciple making and mentoring:

- Begin actively praying with your new believers. It is important that you allow the Holy Spirit to guide this process. You cannot disciple someone who is not ready or willing to be a disciple.

- Find someone to hold you accountable to doing this.

For those who are not being intentionally discipled and mentored:

- Begin actively praying and looking for a trustworthy, reliable person who will commit to you and your spiritual journey.

Choosing "One Another" instead of "One over the Other"

Part of the discipleship process is learning to love one another the way Christ loves us. There are many "one another" verses throughout the New Testament. We are to pray for each other, confess sins, serve, teach, etc. As you grow together in your discipling relationship, and as an MC, consider the "one anothers" to build edifying relationships.

For the Building up of Relationships

- Love one another- *John 13:34-35, 5:12, 17; Romans 12:10; 1 Thessalonians 4:9; 1 John 3:11, 14, 23; 4:7, 11-12; 2 John 1:5; 1 Peter 1:22*
- Increase our love for one another- *2 Thessalonians 1:3*
- Abound in love for one another- *1 Thessalonians 3:12*
- Love each other deeply- *1 Peter 4:8*
- Fellowship with one another- *1 John 1:7*
- Forgive one another- *Ephesians 3:13; 4:32; Colossians 3:13*
- Greet one another- *Romans 16:16; 1 Corinthians 16:20; 2 Corinthians 13:12; 1 Peter 5:14*
- Wait for one another in communion- *1 Corinthians 11:33*
- Bear one another's sufferings- *1 Corinthians 12:26*

For Serving, Teaching, and Encouraging One Another

- Serve one another with gifts received- *1 Peter 4:10; John 13:14*
- Serve one another in love- *Galatians 5:13*
- Be kind to one another- *1 Corinthians 12:25*
- Bear each other's burdens- *Galatians 6:2*
- Work with one another- *1 Corinthians 3:9; 2 Corinthians 6:1*
- Teach one another- *Colossians 3:16*
- Instruct one another- *Romans 5:14*
- Encourage and exhort one another- *Colossians 3:16; Hebrews 3:13, 10:25-26*
- Speak the truth to one another- *Ephesians 4:25*
- Lay down our lives for each other- *1 John 3:16*
- Build up one another- *1 Thessalonians 4:18, 5:2, 11; 1 Corinthians 14:26*
- Confess our sins and pray for one another- *James 5:16*

For Establishing Unity with One Another

- Honor one another- *Romans 12:10*
- Be of one mind with one another- *2 Corinthians 13:11; Romans 12:16, 15:5*
- Do not criticize one another- *Romans 14:13*
- Do not speak bad about one another- *James 4:11, 5:9*
- Submit to one another- *Ephesians 5:21*
- Be clothed with humility toward one another- *1 Peter 5:5*
- Have patience with one another- *Ephesians 4:2*
- Live in peace with one another- *Matthew 9:50*
- Receive one another with hospitality- *Romans 15:7; 1 Peter 4:9*
- Glorify God with each other- *Romans 15:6*

As you grow in your relationship with God and each other evaluate how you are doing in the "one anothers" and how they contribute to your pursuit of the Great Commission.

Chapter 8
Equipping & Developing Leaders

Expected Outcome: Every Disciple Maker will establish a mentoring lifestyle that effectively equips and develops leaders.

Once an MC is planted, the goal of the disciple maker should be to train and develop leaders from within the MC. In principle, **everyone can lead someone**. There must be a recognition that people are the most valuable part of ministry. A proportionate investment into their development, growth, and maturity is required for the equipping of quality leaders.

The root of leadership multiplication is mentoring. What a disciple sees in the life of his or her mentor will be replicated.

Mentorship of Christ-followers is an ongoing process. As they mature, they develop into leaders. Mentoring takes time. Jesus spent 3 years mentoring his disciples.

Understanding Mentorship

A mentor is a maturing person who is involved in training, coaching and helping encourage someone less mature. This can be done one-on-one or in small groups. Whether they realize it or not, every individual, at any time, has multiple mentors in their life. These mentors model actions and attitudes that lead to reproduction of spiritual and social norms.

Parents mentor us as we learn and understand roles and rules of social interaction. Teachers mentor us in our understanding of authority and submission. Friends mentor us as we consider our life direction and the use of our time.

Even our worldview is greatly impacted by the collective mentorship at the hands of our culture or social community. Pastors and authors mentor us as we listen to and read their communications.

This truth applies to the believing community as well. Each new Christ-follower, disciple, and disciple maker needs to be mentored in the tasks of following and serving Christ by someone more mature than themselves. This is an ongoing process rather than a one-time event. The goal is to learn from those who are further along in whatever area you desire growth.

Take a moment and read *Acts 18:24-28* and consider the impact of mentoring "behind the scenes" can have.

2 Timothy 2:2 "And the things that you have heard from me among many witnesses, commit these to faithful men who will be able to teach others also."

Paul had an ongoing discipleship relationship with a few directly, and many more indirectly. Look at the chart below to visually see the impact of one life.

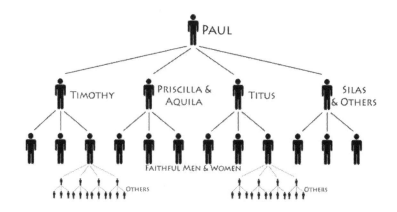

Observations from the Diagram

1. The same leader can start multiple chains.

2. Each generation or "link" in the chain carries a commitment to reproduce and multiply.

3. Faithful men and women are needed to continue the chain.

4. "Others" (4th generation) represent those who will determine the long term passing of the baton of Christianity. Others help ensure that multiplication is the mode of on-going discipleship.

Families are organized in this same fashion. Parents become grandparents when the third generation is born. The goal of your discipleship should be to become a "great grandparent!"

Model & Practice #8.1

Your Paul will now help you create a chart similar to the one above showing the generational links between yourself and your disciples.

- MC leaders often use large, hand-drawn maps to show plans and progress visually. This helps share the vision, monitor progress and assign areas of responsibility.

The task of the **disciple maker** requires reproduction of leaders **on every level**. Expanding the ministry to new and otherwise unreached areas demands the development of people. As stated before, the Gospel spreads through relationships. Intentionality is critical to maintaining and developing any relational goals.

Developing your Timothy's

Paul instructed Timothy to search out those capable of mentoring others, but doing so raises several important areas of consideration (*1 Thessalonians 1:1-2:12; 2 Tim. 2:2*).

Developing Timothys (disciple makers) requires answers to three key questions:

1. How do we identify potential Timothys?
2. What do we train our Timothys to do?
3. How do we mentor our Timothys?

***A wise mentor will listen to their disciple report how their new or potential believers are doing. They will ask for progress updates and work through identified problems.

After assessing the situation, a mentor can effectively challenge and support in a way that addresses current needs and opportunities. The mentor should purposefully assign Scripture reading that supports current actions and follow up on reading done since the last meeting. A good mentor does not simply lecture, they know when to listen and when to talk.

Model & Practice #8.2

Your Paul will now role-play a hypothetical interaction showing how an effective mentor interacts with their disciples.

- After watching, break up into groups of two and practice with each other, taking turns in the mentoring role.

Key Question #1 - How do we identify potential Timothys?

The best place to start is with those you bring to Christ! They are likely to be faithful, accountable, and committed to obeying to the commands of Christ, and willing to be trained and mentored by you. A simple measuring tool for their potential is their level of obedience (*John 14:15*). Give them an opportunity or empower them with a task. Do they do what was assigned? Invest in those who follow through!

It may be cliché, but the proof is in the pudding. Or as Jesus said, people are easily known by their fruit (*Matthew 7:15-20*). As responsibilities are given and fulfilled, the faithful and fruitful come into clarity. Our model for such discernment and selection is Jesus Christ. When the bar is consistently raised, great accomplishments take place.

Something to consider: **Your disciples are unlikely to pray for their disciples more than you pray for yours.** How seriously are you investing in your spiritual harvest? Remember, the key to the harvest is in the harvest.

Multitudes – Followers – Disciples

The end result of Jesus sifting the multitudes was a core of disciples in whom He had deeply invested. From the multitudes, Jesus called for followers. From the followers, Jesus made disciples. From the disciples, He designated apostles to lead the army forward to the nations.

Why is discernment so important?

The greatest resource of the disciple maker is time. Steward your time well. Invest your time in those who will be willing to reproduce and multiply. A simple principle is the 80/20 rule, which suggests one should invest 80% in the top 20%. Have you even considered who might be in your top 20%? Are you investing more heavily in those who are most faithful? It is important to note here that all people matter to God, and this principle is not about ability or talent. Faithfulness and commitment to living on mission with God should be rewarded over productiveness or talent.

Key Question #2 – What do we train our Timothys to do?

Timothys represent the next generation of disciple makers. This means we should mentor our Timothys to do everything expected in the life of a disciple. The leadership development circle introduced above is a simple and practical way to take them through this process, whatever the topic may be.

Something to consider: Moving from generation to generation is a critical aspect of sustaining a movement of disciple makers. As you evaluate who you are training and what you are training them to do, never forget your personal intimacy with Jesus. It has been said, **if you stop** following Jesus personally, you are no longer a disciple, you are simply a salesman. The world does not need more salesmen...it needs more disciples!

Key Question #3 – How do we mentor our Timothys?

Learning can take place in a classroom, but mentoring happens best elsewhere. Just as Jesus and Paul did, we must be willing to walk with our disciples. **It is real-life experience that creates the most value in mentorship.** Application of principles taught, accomplishment of goals set, and the facing of real life problems are all best learned in real life experiences (*1 Corinthians 11:1*). Take your Timothys with you to do ministry. Do more than teach theory. Show them how. **Remember, all training happens in ministry, not just for ministry!**

When you are with your Timothy, be intentional to consider how you can add value to their life. A great mentoring philisophy is to leave things better than you found them. Always consider spiritual growth and remember to include new responsibilities and assignments designed around their needs. Keep in mind as growth happens, the responsibility to determine the next goals and actions will naturally transfer from mentor to mentee.

Everything taught should be practiced to ensure reproducibility in every setting. Christ was an expert mentor. The Lord Himself first modeled those things He expected of His disciples. At times, Jesus would watch from a distance as His disciples were sent out to apply specific lessons. Ultimately, the Lord left the task to His disciples, in full confidence that they would take up the leadership roles He had commissioned for them. Remember, **when you delegate authority along with responsibility, trust is built and people will take action!**

Keys to Mentoring:

- Model skills.
- Meet regularly.
- Pray together and be a source of encouragement.
- Listen carefully to what is said and unsaid.
- Emphasize simple, loving, childlike obedience to Christ.
- Hold accountable and help plan what to do next.
- Help strategize on short-term and long-term objectives.
- Recommend studies that support development, and deal with actual felt needs.
- Help network with other leaders

Model & Practice #8.3

Your Paul will now go through the keys to mentoring with you to see how you are doing. Evaluate your own mentoring efforts.

Chapter 9
Evaluation and Accountability

Expected Outcome: Every disciple maker will support their disciples with intentional evaluation and accountability.

Read *Psalm 145:4* and discuss the following question: **How does what we are doing today impact 100 years from now?**

Evaluation, in our context, means knowing those we disciple deeply and using discernment about their personal life and ministry. The ultimate aim in our relationship with God is to live in a love relationship that brings Him glory while at the same time growing continually as Christ-like leaders.

However, sometimes it is easy to fall into a trap of doing things for God and neglect being with God.

Read *Luke 2:41-45* and discuss the following statements:
- While doing religious duties, it is possible to lose sight of Jesus.
- You can leave Jesus behind without even realizing it.

Before going further, examine your own life and determine if you have fallen prey to any of the above identifed traps. Take some time to pray together as a group.

Purpose of Evaluation: is to ensure the holistic development of the leader/disciple maker is taking place. We are sometimes uncomfortable when trying to measure ministry results. Why do you think that is? When thinking about diagnosing the health of a disciple there are important measurements that identify how we are doing and whether we are growing in a healthy manner.

71

If the goal is to continually grow and move forward in our relationship with God, we must evaluate from time to time whether we ourselves and our disciples are succeeding in the mission given by God.

The defining marks of success for this training include:
- **Living in a love relationship with God.**
- **Growing continually as Christ-like leaders.**
- **Reproducing disciple making leaders.**
- **Planting multiplying MC's.**

Use this framework to measure the success of your efforts and those of your disciples.

Evaluating Quality: this kind of evaluation is helpful to strengthen the character of a disciple maker, which should increase their love for God, their obedience to His commands, and aid in their growth as a Christ-like leader.

Consider for a moment how Jesus evaluated the twelve disciples after He sent them out (*Mark 6:7-10*). In *Mark 6:30* it says the disciples "gathered together with Jesus; and reported to Him all that they had done and taught." Jesus' response was to get away with them to spend some quality time. Such a personal touch and concern even for the fact that they must have been hungry, is a great example to follow today. **As you evaluate your disciples, remember to consider both physical and spiritual needs as both are important!**

Checklist and Questions for Evaluation:

Christ-Centered- Love the Lord (*Matthew 22:37*)
- How is their relationship with Christ?
- Do they spend time with God on a regular basis?
- Do they meditate regularly on God's Word?
- Do they demonstrate the fear of God in their life?

72

Others-Centered- Love your neighbor (*Matthew 22:39*)
- How is their relationship with their family and friends?
- How is their relationship with their fellow leaders?
- How is their relationship with their MC members?
- How is their reputation in the community?
- Do they have a broken relationship with fellow leaders? What is being done to reconcile differences or mend broken relationships?

Character-Love integrity (*1 Timothy 3:1-13; Titus 1:5-9*)
- Do they have a good reputation?
- Are they faithful, honest, and trustworthy?
- Are they humble and reflect Christ's nature in their talk, behavior, and attitudes?
- Do they model self-control?
- How do they react in the middle of crisis or conflict?
- Is there a lifestyle of accountability?

Evaluating what it will take to reach the lost: this kind of evaluation is helpful when addressing the needs of reproducing disciple makers and multiplying MC's.

Compassion- Love the Lost (*Matthew 9:36; Mark 6:34*)
- Is there a brokenness for the lost?
- What does their compassion for others compel them to do?
- Do they delight in the Lord and in keeping His commands?

Competence- Love Truth (*1 Tim. 5:17, 18; 2 Tim. 2:3-7*)
- Do they understand and apply Scripture in their life, and are they able effectively handle the Word of God?
- Are they able to lead?
- Do they desire to grow in the areas required for MC development?

- Do they have the competency for the ministry God has called them?
- Do they self-evaluate and are they willing to make necessary changes?

Model & Practice #9

Your Paul will now go through the above checklist with you.

- As you work your way through the list keep in mind your own disciples and how you are helping them grow and develop.

What's Next?

Congratulations! Working through this manual was not easy! The impact you are having in the Kingdom is remarkable. You are a highly effective leader in a blossoming movement of God. Great care and attention needs to be given to the growing harvest.

You now have a rising number of disciple makers and MC's. If you have not already, you must quickly figure out how to mobilize these disciple makers and MC's into something that is organized and will continue towards maturity and multiplication. We want to help in that process!

There are a few ways to go forward, but whatever you choose there must be an intentional effort to continually develop yourself and those you lead. The growing ministry you have started will require higher levels of leadership for all involved.

We are working on *Disciples Making Disciples Level 3* that will address a lot of the specifics issues that rise as you move from planting individual MC's to leading a growing network of MC's. Some of the topics include:

- How do you go from being an MC planter to an MC multiplier?
- How do you get exposure to other fruitful practices and connected to more specific coaching and mentoring?
- What are the critical skills, values, and time allocations for someone in a multiplier role?
- Are you growing at a pace that will keep up with the growth of those you are leading?

Additional Discovery Bible Study Lessons

Discovering Leadership

Leaders Call Others to Follow Christ *Matthew 4:18-25*

Leaders Teach Healthy Attitudes *Matthew 5:1-16, 6:33-34*

Leaders Seek to Please God *Matthew 6:1-8, 16-18*

Leaders Serve God *Matthew 6:19-34*

Leaders Judge Righteously *Matthew 7:1-6, 18:15-20*

Leaders Seek God *Matthew 7:7-12*

Leaders Obey God *Matthew 7:21-29*

Leaders Care for Outcasts and Sinners *Matthew 9:9-13*

Leaders Teach, Preach, and Heal *Matthew 9:35-38*

Leaders Send People Out *Matthew 10:1-16*

Leaders Prepare for Persecution *Matthew 10:16-31*

Leaders Offer Rest to the Weary *Matthew 11:25-30*

Leaders Teach About the Kingdom *Matthew 13:1-9, 18-23*

Leaders Accept the Cost Matthew 16:13-28

Leaders Listen to Jesus *Matthew 17:1-13*

Leaders Teach About Faith *Matthew 18:15-35*

Leaders Deal with Sin *Matthew18:15-35*

Leaders Honor Marriage *Matthew 19:3-9*

Leaders are Servants *Matthew 20:20-28*

Discovering Church Planting

Love and Obedience *Matthew 22:24-40*

Love and Obedience *Deuteronomy 6:1-6*

Love and Obedience *John 14:15-26*

The Great Commission *Matthew 28:16-20*

Draw People to Christ *John 12:20-33*

Draw People to Christ *John 20:21*

Draw People to Christ *Philippians 2:1-11*

Draw People to Christ *1 Corinthians 9:1-27*

Overcoming Barriers I *Acts 10:9-48*

Overcoming Barriers II *Acts 1:8*

Overcoming Barriers III *Matthew 28:18-20*

Overcoming Barriers IV *Acts 17:15-34*

Overcoming Barriers V *Mark 16:15-16*

Overcoming Barriers VI *Acts 28:1-10*

Overcoming Barriers VII *Luke 24:45-49*

Overcoming Barriers VIII *Luke 24:13-27*

Overcoming Barriers IX *John 20:21*

Overcoming Barriers X *Acts 13:1-4*

Overcoming Barriers XI *John 18:15-27*

Overcoming Barriers XII *John 21:15-19*

Spiritual Warfare I *Ephesians 6:10-18*

Spiritual Warfare II *2 Chronicles 20:1-30*

Spiritual Warfare III *Exodus 17:8-16*

Spiritual Warfare IV *Matthew 24:9-14*

Imitate Christ I *1 Corinthians 4:1-17*

Imitate Christ II *1 Corinthians 10:31-11:1*

Person of Peace I *Luke 9:1-6*

Person of Peace II *Luke 10:1-20*

Appropriate Evangelism I *Matthew 10:5-20*

Appropriate Evangelism II *Acts 16:11-15*

Spiritual Community I *Matthew 28:19-20*

Spiritual Community II *1 Corinthians 12:12-20*

Spiritual Community III *Matthew 16:13-21*

Spiritual Community IV *Acts 2:41-47*

Leadership I *Ezekiel 34*

Leadership II *1 Peter 5:1-11*

Leadership III *Matthew 23:1-39*

Functions of Church *1 Chronicles 16:7-36*

Discovering Obedience

Obedience in the Face of Temptation *Luke 4:1-13*

Obedience to Jesus' Calling *Luke 5:1-11*

Obedience in Telling Others about Christ *John 4:28-30*

Obedience in Evangelizing *Acts 17:16-34*

Obedience in the Power of the Holy Spirit *Acts 4:23-31*

Obedience in Persecution *Acts 21:1-14*

Obedience to a Call in Ministry *Acts 18:1-11*

Obedience in Repentance *Luke 15: 11-32*

Obedience in Inward Purity *Mark 7:14-23*

Obedience in Marriage *Matthew 19:1-12*

Obedience in Generosity *Acts 5:1-11*

Obedience to Respect Government Officials *1 Samuel 24*

Obedience in Radical Love *Matthew 5:43-48*

Obedience in Confession of Sin *Luke 18:9-14*

Obedience in Confession of Sin *Matthew 26:39-42*

Foundational Discipleship Stories

The Shepherd and His Sheep *John 10:22-30*

The Prodigal Son *Luke 15:11-24*

Abiding in Christ *John 15:1-17*

Prayer *Matthew 6:5-15*

Fellowship *Acts 2:41-47*

Being a Witnesses *Acts 1:3-9*

The Greatest Commandment *Mark 12:28-34*

Parable of the Soils *Matthew 13:3-8, 18-23*

Parable of the Talents *Matthew 25:14-30*

Parable of the Persistent Widow *Luke 18:2-8*

Parable of the New and Old *Luke 5:36-38*

Cost of Discipleship *Luke 14:25-33*

Samaritan Woman at the Well *John 4:7-45*

Boldness in the Face of Persecution *Acts 4:23-31*